Italian Consortium for
Pecorino Romano cheese

PECORINO ROMANO CHEESE
THE TASTIEST
STORY
IN THE WORLD

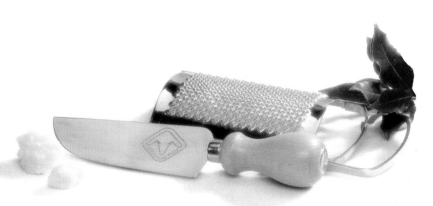

Italian Ministry of Agricultural, Food and Forest Resources

Marco Guarnaschelli Gotti is a journalist at present food critic for "Panorama", an Italian weekly magazine. After obtaining a degree in Italian literature and philosophy, he worked in the theater as an assistant director. From there, he moved to the cinema and became assistant to director Francesco Rosi, working with him on such important movies as "Mani sulla Città" and "The Mattei Affair". He has directed numerous television documentaries and, in the course of his career, has traveled round the world taking the opportunity to sample local cuisines. In this fashion, he has discovered his vocation as a true gastronome and now writes about food, having passed from a general interest to a specialized study of Italian cooking in particular. In 1984, Guarnaschelli Gotti began work on the "Enciclopedia Gastronomica Illustrata", a monumental volume published in 1990 in Reader's Digest Grandi Opere (Great Works) series. He is the author of "Ricette dei Ristoranti d'Italia", a book of restaurant recipes in Italy, and also "Storia della Cucina Milanese" that describes the specialities of Milanese cooking, both published by Franco Muzzio. Since 1987, he has edited the "Cultura Regionale" series for the G.Muzzio publishing group.

Lidia Bastianich is widely regarded as the "First Lady" of Italian restaurants in the United States. Born of ethnic Italian parentage in Pula, Istria, a region formed by the Gulf of Trieste at the juncture of Italy and the former Yugoslavia, Lidia came to New York in 1958. She has left an indelible mark on the city as food historian, executive chef and co-owner of two New York restaurants, FELIDIA and BECCO. Through her restaurants, yearly travels in Italy, lectures and cookbooks, Lidia is credited with having helped bring "authentic" Italian cooking to the American public.

Lidia is a highly respected chef who, having learned the secrets of Italian cooking at her grandmother's knee, expanded her skills through extensive studies and first-hand experience. In her book, LA CUCINA DI LIDIA (Doubleday 1990), she has assembled a collection of 120 simple but sophisticated family recipes that is spiced with tidbits of history and traditions of her homeland and warmed with memories of her family.

Lidia has taught courses in the anthropology of food and is a frequent guest lecturer on the history of Italian cuisine. She has also been a guest chef on the following television programs:
- New York's Master Chef (PBS)
- The Frugal Gourmet (PBS)
- Good Morning America (ABC)
- Regis and Kathy Lee (Syndicated)
- Julia Child's Cooking with Master Chefs (PBS)
- Burt Wolf's Eating Well (PBS)

THE RECIPES

Elegant eating with an extra exciting touch
Recipes created by Lidia Bastianich

The flavor of tradition
Classic Pecorino Romano recipes

The sweets

Joggers in New York's Central Park faltered in their tracks for an instant and rubbed their eyes in amazement when on 26th September 1992, they saw grazing on the grass in front of them a flock of sheep herded by shepherds dressed in their usual working clothes. Sheep in the heart of the Big Apple can cause a sensation. To a New Yorker, recent movies and art exhibitions have made dinosaurs more familiar than sheep and few people know that that particular corner of Central Park is called Sheep Meadow or that, until 1934, genuine New York sheep regularly grazed there.

"grazing on the grass in front of them a flock of sheep. Sheep in the heart of the Big Apple can cause a sensation!"

This surprising pastoral event in 1992, was part of a publicity campaign promoting a pure sheep's milk cheese called "Pecorino" (pecora is the Italian word for sheep) described as being "Romano" or Roman; but apart from the immediate success of the promotion it sometimes happens that good ideas set in motion interesting associations as well as meaningful symbolic values.

Above all, even if for Mediterranean peoples it goes without saying that the sheep as a milk-producing animal is also a producer of cheese, this is not so for the populations of Northern Europe and for the cultures they have spread throughout the world. On the

Sheep Meadow in Central Park N.Y., September '92

> *several major European cities have zones usually in the older districts that take their names from sheep and shepherds*

contrary, even if we are consumers of woolen textiles and sheep meat, we moderns are far from familiar with or respectful towards sheep in general. So it might not be a bad idea to refresh the so-called "historic memory."

Apart from the "pasture" already mentioned in New York, several major European cities have zones usually in the older areas that take their names from sheep and shepherds. In London, for example, there is Shepherd's Market, a small square off Curzon Street close to Mayfair which until the end of the 18th century, as its name implies, was the place where shepherds traded their products right in the heart of the city. And who can forget the Moulin Rouge, fulcrum of Parisian night life situated on the fringe of a particular area still today called Cité Bergère, or the district of the shepherds, next to Faubourg Montmartre, one of the most countrified neighborhoods of Paris where until a few years ago I remember there were vines and orchards on the high ground surrounded by apartment blocks. The Cité Bergère was the home of flocks of sheep and their minders restricted to a small space according to a special statute granted by Paris city hall.

And there is yet another indication of the close connection between sheep raising and the development of human civilization itself: no culture has taboos forbidding the consumption of lamb or mutton, or against sheep's milk and its bi-products. Even the Jewish tradition ("Don't boil the baby in the mother's milk": Deuteronimus 14,21) does not forbid the separate consumption of sheep flesh or milk products but only their association (any meat with any milk product). Having established the nobility of the sheep in our culture, it should be stressed that it is an extraordinarily modern animal in the sense that its life style, its breeding and nutrition correspond to the natural conditions currently considered desirable

regarding everything that concerns us, and which we also expect in the raising of animals.

Flock of sheep grazing on the island of Sardinia

Sheep, especially in the Mediterranean basin, stem from a most ancient and traditional stock, having undergone little crossing and almost no genetic manipulation (unlike cattle such as certain species born without horns or milking cows "pressured" into producing 50 liters of milk a day), meaning that sheep have partaken of a minimum of drugs for their health. Sheep live outdoors, graze on "natural" grass and move around from summer to winter pastures so as to follow the growth cycle from highlands to lowlands and vice versa. This provides the animal with grass having differing characteristics, and this can be detected in the flavor of the milk according to the season of the year. So, for the sheep, no hormones, no diet integrators, no feeding stuff panels, no pharmaceutical cocktails: just fresh air, grass and the sky overhead.

" another interesting aspect of this special cheese concerns its preservation, a process that took place before Pecorino Romano found its way into the cookery books "

Coming to the milk. Sheep's milk has a higher percentage of fat, nitrogenous substances and mineral salts compared with cows' milk and has a characteristic flavor due in part to the animal itself and partly to the variety of grasses it has consumed. When we talk about pecorino cheese, it is important to know its production period as well as the region it comes from: cheeses made from other milks reflect their origins with less precision than pecorino which imprints its characteristics with DNA-like precision.

In Italy, Spain and France, sheep's milk is used exclusively to make cheese: while in Greece and the Balkans it is used to make other products like kaimak and yoghurt.

Pecorino Romano has to be considered from its gastronomic point of view and for its nutritional content of proteins, fats and mineral salts. Another interesting aspect of this special cheese concerns its preservation, a process that took place some time before it found its way into the cookery books. Cooking the cheese enormously helped its preservation even if the early rudimental "scorching" said little from the gastronomic point of view while those who were familiar with the fresh cheese probably still liked it better uncooked. Then, after the discovery

" in olden times as the human race desperately struggled for survival, cheese played an important role "

of salt deposits, sheep's milk cheese acquired further changes when it was cured with salt, or smoked, and finally by the combination of various techniques.

In olden times, as the human race desperately struggled for survival, cheese played an important role and was one of the most ancient forms of food. There is nothing that goes bad quicker than milk and day after day prehistoric man witnessed this catastrophe happening to a precious foodstuff that he had already learned to appreciate.

Then, something happened that changed everything and, in this connection, we can accept the following Arab legend as being probably not far from the truth. It relates

how a shepherd from the countryside had to make a journey taking with him a quantity of milk. To conveniently carry the liquid, he had the idea of putting it in a bag made from a goat's stomach tied at one end. Much to his amazement, this milk turned to curds and whey due to the churning movement of the container.

Filled with curiosity, he tentatively sampled the soft white gobs only to find them pleasant to the taste. In this simple way, cheese was born.

Lengthy experimentation followed in order to establish basic cheese-making procedure and the various methods necessary to obtain quality and different characteristics.

Several thousands of years later, we learn some facts about the art of cheese-making from reading Homer's "Odyssey" written some 700 years before Christ, as told by one-eyed Poliphemus. Since the Cyclops was neither an intellectual nor an experimenter, when he informs Ulysses about the technique of curdling milk to produce cheese, we presume that by then the process was common knowledge even among the most ignorant of shepherds. And the cheeses in question were made from the milk of sheep and goats. Pastures were scarce in the Mediterranean basin in those days and cows were able to forage only enough grass to provide milk for their calves. So man had to go elsewhere for his cheese as we have seen.

Eight centuries after Homer, Latin agronomist Lucio Moderato Columella writing in the De Re Rustica tract, laid down certain fixed rules for cheese-making using sheep's milk. He wrote: "Generally speaking, the milk is curdled using rennet from lambs or baby goats, or even by using thistle flowers, safflower or the milky juice of figs. Then

" Eight centuries after Homer, a Latin agronomist laid down certain fixed rules for cheese-making using sheep's milk "

11

" around two thousand years later, Pecorino Romano, is the best-known and most exported of all Italian cheeses "

the milk in the bucket must be kept at medium heat but not placed close to the fire as some say, but nearby and, as soon as the milk curdles, the curds must be put into baskets, molds or other receptacles. It is essential that the whey be drained off immediately so that it is separated from the solid curds.

It is for this reason that the peasant farmers do not wait for the liquid to ooze out gradually, but as soon as the curds are somewhat solid, they place weights on top so as to squeeze out the whey. When the solidified mass is removed from the baskets or molds, in order not to deteriorate it must be placed on clean tables in a cool, dark place and sprinkled with fine salt so as to sweat out its acid moisture."

And what cheese did the Bishop of Vabres offer Charlemaine on his return from the Spanish expedition six centuries later? A sort of Roquefort made from sheep's milk.

Cows' milk cheese was certainly known by that time but it is only seriously talked about after the year 1,000 A.D.

Around two thousand years later, Pecorino Romano, the best-known and most exported of all Italian cheeses, is still made in that

continues on page 34

Elegant eating with an extra exciting touch

Recipes created by Lidia Bastianich

Ricotta dumplings in radicchio sauce

Serves 6

1 lb ricotta cheese
1/2 tsp pepper
2 cups flour, plus more as needed
1/4 tsp ground nutmeg
2 eggs, beaten
3/4 tsp salt
1 tsp chopped Italian parsley
1/2 cup grated Pecorino Romano

Drain the ricotta over-night in a sieve. Make a well in the 2 cups flour and add the ricotta, eggs, salt, Pecorino Romano, spices, and parsley. Gradually in-corporate the elements until a soft dough forms, adding more flour if the mixture is sticky.

With 2 spoons well floured make dum-plings and drop them in 4 quarts lightly sal-ted boiling water until the dumplings rise to the surface, about 7 minutes. Drain imme-diately and set in plate with sauce.

Meanwhile make the Radicchio Trevisano Sauce

2 tbs olive oil
2 whole large heads of radicchio Trevisano, sliced thin crosswise
1 cup onion, diced
1 cup good chicken stock
1/2 cup dry white wine
1 tbs fresh mint leaves, chopped
1 cup grated Pecorino Romano
1/2 cup Pecorino Romano shavings
Salt and pepper to taste

Sweat the onion in the oil, add sliced radic-chio and simmer until wilted. Add wine and let evaporate, salt and pepper to taste and stock a little at a time simmering the sauce till done, 15 to 20 minutes.

Add the mint, mix and spoon onto hot dum-plings adding grated Pecorino Romano and decorating with shav-ings of the same cheese.

Potato dough ribbon pasta with artichokes and Pecorino Romano

Serves 6

6 large Idaho or russet potatoes
2 tbs plus 1 tsp salt
Dash of freshly ground white pepper
4 cups unbleached flour
1/4 cup Pecorino Romano
2 eggs, beaten

Boil the potatoes in their skins about 40 minutes, until easily pierced with a skewer. When cool enough to handle, peel and dice the potatoes, and set them aside to cool completely, spreading them loosely to expose as much surface as possible to air.

Before proceeding further, bring 6 qts water and 2 tbs of the salt to a boil.

On a cool, preferably marble work surface, gather the cold diced potatoes into a mound, forming a well in the center. Stir the remaining 1 tsp salt and the white pepper into the beaten eggs and pour the mixture into the well. Work the potatoes and eggs together with both hands, gradually adding 3 cups of the flour and scraping the dough up from the work surface with a knife as often as necessary.

Dust the dough, your hands, and the work surface lightly with flour and cut the dough into four equal parts and roll out to 1/8" thickness, then cut strips 1"x 4" to form "pappardelle".

Continue to dust dough, hands, and surface while working the dough.

Drop the pappardelle into salted boiling water a few at a time, stirring gently and continuously with a wooden spoon, and cook 2-3 minutes, until they rise to the surface. Remove the pappardelle from the water with a slotted spoon or skimmer, drain well, transfer them to a warm platter, adding a little sauce, and boil the remaining pieces in batches until all are done.

Meanwhile make the Artichoke Sauce

5 medium artichokes
4 tbs olive oil
5 cloves of garlic, crushed
1/4 cup chopped Italian parsley
2 cups tasty chicken stock
1/2 cup grated Pecorino Romano
Salt and pepper to taste

Clean the artichokes by peeling off tough outer leaves, then cut off 1/4 of the artichoke, the spiny tips, with a chopping knife. Cut the artichoke in half vertically and with a pairing knife remove the beard and any tough leaves. Set cleaned artichokes in 1 quart of cold water

and the juice of 2
lemons to prevent
discoloration, then pro-
ceed to cut each half
vertically in thin slices.

Cook the garlic in 3 tbs
of olive oil till golden,
add the drained arti-
choke slices, salt, pep-
per, and simmer by
adding small amounts
of stock. Simmer for 15
minutes leaving enough
sauce to coat the pasta.
Add the cooked pap-
pardelle, drizzle with
remaining olive oil and
parsley, toss gently
with wooden spoon,
sprinkle with Pecorino
Romano and serve.

Pasticciata with herbs, tomato and fresh spinach sauce

Serves 8

Crepes

2 eggs
1 cup milk
2 cups water
1/2 cup club soda
1/4 cup sugar
1/4 tsp salt
2 1/2 cups flour
6 tbs melted butter
Grated zest of 1 lemon
Vegetable oil, for frying

In a bowl, whisk the eggs. Add the milk, club soda, sugar, water, salt and blend well. Gradually sift in the flour to form a batter, then stir in the melted butter. (The consistency should be that of melted ice cream). Add the lemon zests. In a large crepe pan, heat 1 tbs vegetable oil over moderately high flame, pouring off the excess. Tilt the heated and oiled pan at a 45° angle and pour batter in small batches into the pan, allowing it to run down from the highest point (usually a ladleful of batter will cover the pan adequately).

Return the pan to the heat, reduce the flame to moderate, and cook the crepe until lightly browned, about 30-40 seconds. Flip it carefully with a spatula and cook the second side.

Remove from the pan and repeat the process with the remaining batter, re-oiling the pan only as necessary.

Bechamelle

3-1/2 cups milk
at room temperature
2 bay leaves
Pinch of nutmeg
6 tbs unsalted butter
1/2 cup all-purpose flour
Salt and freshly ground
white pepper

In a small saucepan, combine the milk, bay leaves and nutmeg and bring to a simmer over moderate heat.

Meanwhile, in a heavy medium saucepan, melt the butter. Stir in the flour and cook over moderate heat, mixing frequently, until smooth and light in color, about 1 minute. Gradually whisk in the milk until smooth. Cook over low heat, whisking frequently, until the sauce thickens and no floury taste remains, about 10 minutes. Strain the sauce and season with salt and pepper to taste.

Stuffing

1-1/2 lbs ricotta cheese
1/2 lb mascarpone
2 cups grated Pecorino Romano
2 eggs
2 cups cooked and finely minced Swiss chard or spinach
1 tbs salt
Freshly ground pepper
Bunch scallions,
leeks, fresh sage, basil, thyme
Blend all the stuffing ingredients well to assemble
1 cup Pecorino Romano

Butter well an 8" x 10" ceramic or glass baking dish and line it with the crepes letting all the ends overlap 2" over the baking dish edge.

Spread some of the white sauce evenly over the crepes, then spread spinach stuffing, some sauce and cover with crepes.

Sprinkle Pecorino Romano, continue to alternate with crepes, bechamelle, stuffing, crepes and so on finishing with bechamelle. Cover with crepes, fold the hanging flaps of crepes over the pasticciata sealing it for baking.
Reserve 1 cup of bechamelle, and 2 cups of parmesan. Dress the top with cheese and bake at 450 for 30 minutes.
Let cool for 15 minutes, cut into squares and serve.

Spinach sauce

1 lb spinach leaves, cleaned, washed and steamed
3 tbs butter
Salt and fresh pepper
1/4 cup heavy cream
1/2 cup chicken stock

Sauté steamed spinach in butter; season, add cream and half the stock. Let simmer for 2 minutes. Pass in the food processor till smooth, if too dense add remaining stock.

Tomato sauce

12 ripe plum tomatoes
2 tbs minced shallots
3 tbs olive oil
Salt, pinch of crushed red pepper
Freshly ground black pepper
4 leaves of fresh basil

Bring a large saucepan of water to a full boil. Drop in the tomatoes and leave them 15 seconds. Remove with a slotted spoon and drop in iced water. When cool, peel off skin with a paring knife. Core, halve, and gently squeeze out seeds reserving the juice. Chop tomatoes and set aside.

Sauté the minced shallots in oil without browning. Add tomato pulp, juice and seasoning and cook over moderately high heat for 5 minutes.

Remove basil leaves, pass in a processor till smooth.

Spread each half of plate with different sauce and set pasticciata in center with sprig of basil as decoration.

𝒲edding 𝒫asta

Serves 8

Dough

3 whole eggs plus
1 yolk
2-1/2 cups flour
1/4 tsp salt

Beat the eggs, yolk, and
salt well. Sift the flour,
forming a mound, and
make a well in the cen-
ter. Add the eggs and
mix with your fingers
until the dough comes
together. Knead until
soft and pliable, adding
flour, 1 tbs at a time, if

dough feels sticky; or water, 1 tsp at a time, if dry and crumbly. Knead the dough for about 10 minutes until smooth and elastic, or use the food processor. Cover with plastic wrap and let the dough rest while preparing stuffing.

Stuffing

1/2 cup golden raisins
2 tbs dark rum
2 eggs, beaten with pinch of salt
1/2 lb Fontina cheese, shredded
1/4 lb freshly grated parmesan
1/4 lb Pecorino Romano
1/4 cup bread crumbs
1/2 tsp grated lemon zest
1/2 tsp grated orange zest
1/2 tsp sugar

Soak the raisins in the rum. In a large bowl, beat together the eggs and sugar. Add Fontina, parmesan, and bread crumbs, mixing well. Add the remaining ingredients and combine well, using your hands. Cover and set aside.

Assemble the krafi

Divide the dough into three parts and roll out each part to form a rectangle about 1/16" thick. If using a pasta machine, pass the dough through successively narrower openings, ending with the next to-thinnest setting. (Keep the remaining dough covered while working each portion). Set the rolled dough on a work surface with the long side facing you and spoon the filling onto the upper (farthest) half, by the tablespoonful, at 3" intervals. Lightly moisten the dough with water along the edges and around the mounds of filling. Fold unfilled bottom half of dough over the top, aligning the borders, and press around the mounds and along the edges to seal. Using a round cookie cutter, stamp out the krafi. Press each filled portion lightly to fill the air pockets with stuffing, check the edges to be sure they are completely sealed, and set the krafi on a floured cloth. Repeat the procedure until the filling is used up .
Boil the krafi in a large pot of salted water until "al dente" but cooked through, 6-8 minutes. Drain, toss well with 2/3 cup melted unsalted butter, sprinkle liberally with grated Pecorino Romano and serve with freshly ground pepper and additional Pecorino Romano.

Grilled halibut flavored with herbs and Pecorino Romano in a tomato sauce

Serves 4

1-1/2 lbs fillet of halibut, cut into 4 slices
1-1/2 cups fresh bread crumbs
1 tsp thyme, finely minced
1 tsp oregano, finely minced
6 basil leaves, reserve 4 sprigs for decoration, finely minced
4 tbs grated Pecorino Romano
4 tbs olive oil
Salt and pepper to taste

Salt and pepper then coat the halibut with 2 tbs of olive oil, set on a baking sheet and bake in a preheated oven (450° F.) for 60 mins. Mix well the bread crumbs, herbs, 2 tbs olive oil, salt and pepper, divide in four parts and with a spoon cover evenly the top of each fish. Pat down lightly with end of spoon and return to oven for an additional 10 minutes.

Tomato sauce

Yields 2-1/2 cups
2-1/2 lbs ripe plum tomatoes
1/2 tsp pepper flakes and salt
1 cup minced onion
3 tbs olive oil
8 fresh basil leaves, minced
16 Gaeta olives, pitted & cut in half

With the point of a pairing knife cut out and discard the stem bases of the tomatoes.

Bring water to boil in a large saucepan, drop in the tomatoes, and cook 5 minutes. With a slotted spoon, transfer the tomatoes to a colander, run cold water over them, and slip their skins off with your fingers. Squeeze tomatoes over a strainer removing seeds and reserving the juice.

In a non-reactive saucepan, lightly sauté the onion in the olive oil. Add the tomatoes, crushing each directly over the pan as it is added. Add the reserved juice, pepper flakes, season to taste and simmer 20 minutes, stirring occasionally, then pass through a sieve. Ladle tomato sauce to cover base of each plate, set roasted halibut in center position, with olives and diced tomatoes around the fish, and decorate with fresh basil.

Stuffed calamari

Serves 4

8 medium size calamari, cleaned, chop the tentacles and reserve
1 egg
1/2 cup shredded carrots
1/2 cup bread crumbs
1 cup Pecorino Romano, grated
6 cloves of garlic, sliced
1/2 cup parsley, minced
2 tbs shallots
4 tbs olive oil
1/2 cup dry white wine
Salt & pepper to taste

Sauté the shallots in 2 tbs olive oil, then add tentacles and carrots, season and simmer for 5 minutes. Remove from heat and let cool, then add the egg, the bread crumbs, the Pecorino Romano, 1/4 cup parsley, salt & pepper, and mix well. Stuff each sac with the mixture and seal with a toothpick. In a skillet sauté the garlic in remaining olive oil till golden, set the stuffed calamari side by side, season with salt and pepper and cook over moderate heat, stirring and turning occasionally.
When skillet begins to get dry, add wine and cook for 5 minutes, then add 1/4 cup of water and cook until sauce is syrupy, optional remove garlic, sprinkle with remaining parsley and serve.

Grilled veal chop decorated with spinach and Pecorino Romano

Serves 4

4 veal chops, 1"to 1-1/2"
thick depending on
preference
1 lb whole leaves spinach,
cleaned and washed
5 tbs olive oil
4 cloves of garlic
Salt and pepper
1 cup Pecorino Romano,
grated

1 pint cherry tomatoes,
red and yellow halves
4 leaves of fresh basil cut
in strips

Season the veal chops
with salt, pepper and
coat with 2 tbs of olive
oil. Grill veal chops on
hot grill turning on
both sides for 15-18
minutes depending on
heat of grill and the
thickness of the chops.

Meantime, crush the
garlic cloves, divide
the remaining olive oil
and garlic in two pans,
cook till golden. To
one pan add spinach,
salt and pepper and

braise till done, 3-4
minutes, drain pan
juices, remove garlic
cloves and divide spi-
nach evenly over each
chop. Sprinkle with
Pecorino Romano and
set in broiler to crisp
the cheese - if top broi-
ler is not available set
in hot oven for an addi-
tional 5 minutes.

Meanwhile, in other
pan, with garlic sauté
briefly the tomatoes,
adding salt and pepper
to taste and shredded
basil. Remove garlic
cloves. Set veal chops
in plate and flank with
braised tomatoes.

Tomato tartlet with Pecorino Romano

Serves 4

Zest of 1 lemon
2 cups all-purpose flour
1/4 tsp salt
4 tbs unsalted margarine
1/4 lb (1 stick)
unsalted butter
Pecorino Romano, grated
2 leeks
Sliced tomatoes
Approximately 4 tbs ice
water
1 tsp fresh thyme, chopped

Pour flour and salt in bowl of food processor. Cut butter and margarine into small bits, and add to the flour, with lemon zest and thyme. Process 10 seconds, or until mixture resembles coarse meal. Add the water, processing as little as possible (10 to 15 seconds).

Dough should just hold together in the bowl, but not be wet or sticky. Turn out onto plastic wrap, press into a ball, and chill at least 1 hour before using.
Roll out dough on a lightly floured board 1/8" thick and set in buttered 4" tartlet pans. Shape with fingers and cut off excess. Press empty tartlet pan on top to prevent puffing while baking, and set in refrigerator to chill for 30 minutes.
Bake in a 375° F. preheated oven for 15 minutes, remove top pan and return to oven for additional 3-5 minutes and let cool on rack.

Meanwhile prepare the vegetables. Sauté leeks in 2 tbs oil till done, season with salt and pepper and spread on the base of the tartlet, set slices of tomatoes in petal-like fashion, season with salt and pepper, drizzle with remaining oil.
Toss Pecorino Romano with oregano and sprinkle to cover the whole tartlet and return to the hot oven for additional 7 to 10 minutes till golden.
Serve warm, decorate with fresh oregano and drizzle with additional olive oil.

Beet risotto

Serves 4

2 cups Arborio rice
2 red beets, cooked
1 onion, diced
2 tbs shallots, minced
1 qt chicken stock
1 cup dry white wine
2 tbs olive oil
2 tbs butter
5 tbs Pecorino Romano, plus shavings for decoration
Salt and pepper to taste

Peel and dice the cooked beets, set them aside with 1 cup of their liquid.
In a medium casserole, heat olive oil and saute' onion and shallots until golden.
Add rice and stir to coat with oil. Add wine and let evaporate.
Stir well, and add 1/2 cup of the hot chicken stock and salt. Cook, stirring constantly, until all liquid has been absorbed.
Continue to add hot stock in small batches until rice mixture is creamy and "al dente". When the rice is almost ready, add the beets and the reserved liquid, salt and pepper. Remove from heat, amalgamate butter and Pecorino Romano, top with shavings and serve.

Panzanella with Pecorino Romano

Serves 4

1 lb stale Tuscan bread, or country bread with a thick crust that is a few days old and dry
4 large ripe tomatoes, diced
1 large red onion, diced
1 cucumber, seeded, diced
8 leaves of basil, shredded
3 tbs red wine vinegar
4 tbs extra virgin olive oil
Salt and pepper to taste
1 cup Pecorino Romano, shredded

Cut the bread in 1/2" cubes. In a salad bowl, combine the bread with cucumber, onions, tomatoes and basil leaves. Mix dressing, oil and vinegar, salt and pepper, and add to the bowl. Mix well, cover and refrigerate for 30 minutes. Set on a plate, decorate with basil and sprinkle the shredded Pecorino Romano evenly and serve.

Asparagus salad with Pecorino Romano

Serves 4

2 lbs asparagus,
trimmed and peeled
1/2 tsp salt (or to taste)
1 cup Pecorino Romano,
shaved
1 cup ripe tomatoes, diced
3 tbs red wine vinegar
4 tbs olive oil freshly
ground pepper
1/2 lb leaves of mixed
salad of choice
6 basil leaves, cut julienne

In a large pot, steam or boil the asparagus with lightly salted water until just tender, about 6 minutes. Drain immediately in a colander and refresh under cold running water. Pat asparagus dry.

In a bowl blend the vinegar, oil, salt and pepper

Set salad on center of plates. Toss the tomatoes, Pecorino Romano, basil with half of the dressing. Spoon on salad, set the asparagus on top and drizzle remaining dressing over asparagus and salad.

Sweet Pecorino Romano Cheese Fritters

Makes 6-18 pieces

1 cup warm water
1 oz fresh yeast
1/2 cup warm milk
1 tbs sugar
2 cups flour
1 egg
1/4 tsp salt
1/2 tbs baking powder
8 shredded basil leaves
3 cups vegetable oil
1 cup grated Pecorino Romano

Dissolve yeast in warm milk together with the sugar and 1/2 cup of the flour. Mix well (the mixture will resemble lumpy pancake butter), cover and set aside in a warm place to activate the yeast. The mass should double in volume within 15-20 minutes.

In the meantime, beat egg with salt. Combine baking powder with remaining flour and add to mixture. Blend well and add yeast mixture. Beat 10-15 minutes, until dough is soft and sticky. Add to dough, basil leaves, Pecorino Romano and mix well. Cover with a dry cloth and let rise in a warm place until the volume doubles, about 40 minutes. In a deep skillet, heat vegetable oil just short of smoking point. Dip a teaspoon into hot oil then scoop up as much dough as the spoon will hold, and slide it into the hot oil with another oiled spoon. Repeat process until skillet is full. Fry fritters, turning with a slotted spoon, until honey brown on all sides. Drain on paper towels, repeat with remaining dough.

Sauce

3 cups peeled tomatoes
3 tbs bread crumbs
2 tbs olive oil
3 cloves of garlic, crushed
Basil sprigs for decoration and sauce
Salt and pepper to taste

Cook garlic in olive oil till golden, pass tomatoes in a vegetable puree then add to pan, salt and pepper to taste, a few basil leaves and simmer for 15 minutes. Bring to vigorous boiling, add bread crumbs and cook additional 3 minutes, stirring. Pass through a sieve and serve.

Spread tomato sauce covering the base of the whole plate and place the fritters in the center. Grate additional Pecorino Romano over the fritters and decorate with basil sprigs.

Avocado with Pecorino Romano and balsamic vinegar

Serves 4

2 large ripe avocados,
pitted and pealed
3 oz. Pecorino Romano,
cut into shavings
2 tbs olive oil
1 tbs traditional
Balsamic vinegar

Salt and pepper
1 tbs small capers,
drained
4 basil sprigs for
decoration

Cut each avocado in
half and set it on center
of plate. Whisk dressing of oil, vinegar, salt
and pepper to taste and
add capers. Set the
shavings of Pecorino
Romano into the avocado like a porcupine,
spoon dressing on side
of avocado, decorate
with basil and orange
slices and serve.

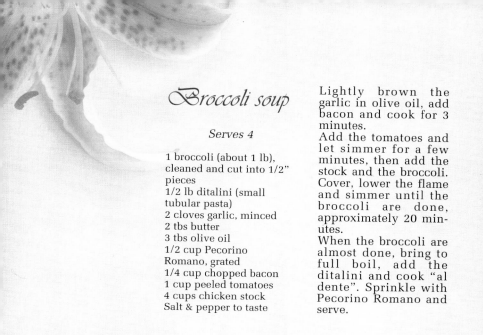

Broccoli soup

Serves 4

1 broccoli (about 1 lb), cleaned and cut into 1/2" pieces
1/2 lb ditalini (small tubular pasta)
2 cloves garlic, minced
2 tbs butter
3 tbs olive oil
1/2 cup Pecorino Romano, grated
1/4 cup chopped bacon
1 cup peeled tomatoes
4 cups chicken stock
Salt & pepper to taste

Lightly brown the garlic in olive oil, add bacon and cook for 3 minutes.

Add the tomatoes and let simmer for a few minutes, then add the stock and the broccoli. Cover, lower the flame and simmer until the broccoli are done, approximately 20 minutes.

When the broccoli are almost done, bring to full boil, add the ditalini and cook "al dente". Sprinkle with Pecorino Romano and serve.

continued from page 12

> ❝ *Pecorino Romano is a modern cheese in its essentialities, its unmistakable flavor, its balanced nutritional qualities* ❞

same way not only by small farmers but also on an industrial scale by dairy product manufacturers, the only differences being, apart from the high hygienic standards required today, that the milk is warmed by means of an electric coil rather than an open fire, standard-size receptacles are used rather than baskets, mechanized equipment rather than by hand ... and little else. Pecorino Romano is a modern cheese in its essentialities, its unmistakable flavor, its balanced nutritional qualities, and the possibility to preserve it in portions without any special requirement.

The following is how Pierre Androuet in "Le Guide du Fromage", the bible of cheeses,

---

THE CHARACTERISTICS OF PECORINO ROMANO CHEESE

Fats: minimum 36% in ratio to the dry bulk

Texture: hard, compressed, half-cooked, white and creamy-white

Rind: Natural, brushed, black or white

Maturation: in cool rooms, minimum aging 5-8 months

Production period: from November to June

To be consumed: all the year round since the cheese remains unaltered once matured

Shape: cylindrical, 25-35 cm. in diameter, height 25-35 cm., weight betweeen 18 and 40 kg.

Characteristics: Appearance: white or black rind, white or creamy-white consistency. Hard and compact to the touch. Odor: fragrant.
Taste: piquant and strongly characteristic.

Normal use: when fresh, as a table cheese; when aged, grated or in flakes, to add flavor to dishes.

---

describes Pecorino Romano:-country of origin: Italy, from the provinces of Rome, Frosinone, Latina, Viterbo, Grosseto, Cagliari, Sassari, Nuoro. In other words, a profile that is brief and to the point but not without a touch of romanticism ("smoked out of doors") from perhaps the greatest of all experts. But Androuet, like all the French, is not particularly generous towards the products of other nations and in fact possesses the dry, essential judgement fitting to a descendent of Voltaire. In other words, we can consider ourselves satisfied.

The outside appearance of Pecorino Romano consists of a cylindrical block with either a white or black rind on which the special trademark of the producers' consortium is stamped. This is in the form of a stylized sheep's head and somewhat resembles the shape of a prehistoric arrow head. The cheese inside is white or creamy-white, the texture is firm and compact but with a grainy surface that seems to invite you to shave off a nugget to nibble. Here and there are tiny little holes which, in the youngest blocks are like little teardrops where the flavor is concentrated.

> *The outside appearance of Pecorino Romano consists of a cylindrical block with either a white or black rind*

Making the curds

The flavor is always piquant tasting more or less of sheep's milk to which the saltiness adds gusto. It is a flavor that cannot be confused with other sheep's milk cheeses, derived from characteristic pastures and from the typical way the cheese is prepared. Without getting too detailed, the most important phases that give the cheese its special charactertistics are the warming of the curds to 120° F., the introduction of long wooden pins while at the same time manually pressing and turning the already-cut blocks in order to accelerate the draining off of the whey, a process that takes less than 30 minutes, and, finally, the curing that is done by hand using dry salt in cool cellars or air-conditioned rooms at temperatures of 58-60° F.

Curing is enormously important because on it depends the technical success of the cheeses. It takes from 80 to 100 days during which time the blocks are hand-turned at first every 24 hours, then every 3 to 4 days, then every 6 days after 45 days have elapsed.

When the curing is over, aging begins with

" aging begins with the cylindrical blocks stored for a minimum of five months on pinewood shelves "

The curing

Pressing

the cylindrical blocks stored for a minimum of five months on pinewood shelves. During this period they are brushed and turned regularly.

Let's briefly recap the typical conditions required for the production of Pecorino Romano cheese. Firstly, comes the quality of the pastures where the sheep graze, then the production phase consisting of the technique, the curing and finally the aging. These conditions interact to give this cheese its principal characteristics: aroma and flavor, excellent keeping and transporting qualities, flexibility of use either in cooking or served at table. These are the conditions prescribed by the Consorzio per la Tutela del Formaggio Pecorino Romano (Consortium for Pecorino Romano Cheese), a private body set up in 1955, composed of the producers themselves in order to ensure the strict observance of the rules of production by those using the brand name.

Binding

So we see that sheep's milk and the cheese made from it accompany mankind from his earliest existence. Cheese is not an obvious product but it represents rather one of the greatest conquests in food-production technology ever achieved by man. You might well ask why a cheese named Pecorino Romano can be produced not only in the Lazio province around Rome but also from Tuscany and the nearby island of Sardinia? Or why the Consortium has its headquarters at Macomer in Sardinia rather

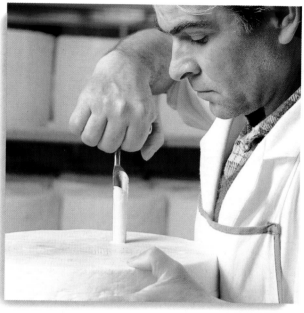

Quality control

than Rome? We will deal with the historical reasons for this later but the most important factor is that the typicality of the cheese is based not on its territorial boundaries but on the characteristics of the pastures, the particular breed of the sheep and, therefore, of the milk they produce. Not all of Latium but only certain zones of the province produce this sheep's milk with the correct organic characteristics necessary for this typical cheese. The same is true of Sardinia since not all the grazing lands there result in a cheese of the desired standards.

Going back for a moment to the many writings of Columella regarding Pecorino Romano, after describing its production method he makes this statement of prophetic importance: "This type of cheese can even travel overseas." In an era when refrigeration or

❝Columella makes this statement of prophetic importance:'This type of cheese can even travel overseas'❞

39

" The whole operation is based on years of experience in which the fundamental phases are still today carried out by hand by craftsmen known by special names that denote their role "

pasteurization did not exist this was something not to be discounted although we do not know how much Pecorino Romano actually did go abroad in those far-off days. But Columella would surely have been proud to have singled out this aspect the cheese that today certainly facilitates the annual exportation of some 45 million pounds, 90% of which goes to the United States and Canada.

However, this ability to travel and keep once it has been aged is only one part of the Pecorino Romano story. The specialized production methods of this cheese allow it to be kept without growing mold or developing other signs of decay. It keeps all its qualities of touch, smell, and taste practically intact and this is very important for the blocks that have been cut open and chopped into portions. Unlike other cheeses, after a few days in the refrigerator Pecorino Romano does not lose its moisture, smell fusty or absorb the smells of other foods. All that is necessary is to wrap it in foil and it will last with all its qualities unaltered.

There is no trick involved, it is just a question of equilibrium between slow curing - with the salt slowly absorbed in the 100-day period so as to become an integral part of the cheese - and a very slow aging process that is not simply a drying-out but rather a state of change in the consistency of the cheese itself. The whole operation is based on years of experience in which the fundamental phases are still today carried out by

continues on page 54

40

The flavor
of tradition

Classic Pecorino Romano recipes

Bucatini all'Amatriciana

(Bucatini pasta, bacon, tomato and Pecorino Romano cheese)

Serves 4

1 lb bucatini pasta
2 cups canned plum tomatoes, chopped
1 cup chopped bacon
2 tablespoons extra virgin olive oil
1 garlic clove
1/2 onion, chopped
1/2 hot pepper, flaked
1/2 cup grated Pecorino Romano cheese
Salt

Chop bacon into cubes and sauté together with garlic and onion. Remove the garlic as soon as it begins to brown, add the hot pepper flakes and the drained and chopped tomatoes. Add salt to taste and cook over a medium heat for 30 minutes, stirring to prevent sticking.

Cook the bucatini pasta until just done in boiling salted water, drain and place in a serving dish. Pour over the tomato sauce, sprinkle with Pecorino Romano cheese and serve immediately.

Rigatoni alla carbonara
(Rigatoni pasta, eggs, bacon and Pecorino Romano cheese)

Serves 4

1 lb rigatoni pasta
1 cup smoked bacon
3 eggs
1/2 cup grated Pecorino Romano
2 tbs extra virgin olive oil
Pepper, freshly ground
Salt

Chop bacon into cubes and sauté slowly in a large pan until the fat is melted.
Cook the rigatoni pasta in a large pan of boiling salted water until just done. Drain and put in the sauté pan with bacon. While the pasta is cooking, mix the eggs and grated cheese in a bowl with a pinch of salt and freshly ground black pepper.
Put this mixture in the sauté pan and toss with the drained rigatoni. Place in a pre-heated serving dish and serve immediately.

43

Penne pasta, broccoli and Pecorino Romano cheese

Serves 4

4 tbs olive oil
4 cloves garlic, thinly sliced
4 cups steamed broccoli, coarsely chopped
1 cup chicken stock
Freshly ground black pepper, to taste
3/4 cup shaved or grated Pecorino Romano
1 lb penne pasta

In a sauté pan, heat the olive oil over medium heat.
Add the garlic and cook for 2 minutes until fragrant. Add the steamed broccoli and sauté for 1 minute. Add the stock, raise the heat, and cook until the liquid is almost evaporated, stirring occasionally.
Bring 5 quarts of salted water to boil and throw in the penne pasta. Cook until just done and drain. Toss the pasta with the broccoli sauce and season to taste with pepper. Add the Pecorino Romano cheese, saving some for serving. Toss again and serve.

Tagliatelle pasta, fava beans and Pecorino Romano cheese

Serves 4

2 lbs unshelled fava beans or one 10-ounce package frozen baby lima beans, thawed
4 tbs extra virgin olive oil
2 medium shallots, finely chopped
Pinch of peperoncino, (hot pepper flakes)
1-1/2 cups chicken stock
Salt and freshly ground black pepper, to taste
1/4 cup grated Pecorino Romano
1 lb tagliatelle pasta

Shell the fava beans and blanch in salted boiling water for 1 minute, drain and immediately plunge into iced water. Peel off the outer skins. If using lima beans, thaw and keep at room temperature. Keep aside 1/2 cup beans. Place the olive oil in a skillet, add the shallots and peperoncino and sauté over a medium-low heat until shallots are wilted. Add stock, increase heat and bring to the boil and cook for 5 minutes. Add beans and salt and pepper, to taste. Cook for 2 minutes.

Blend the mixture in a food processor or blender. Cook pasta until just done, drain and place it in a bowl (keeping aside 1/2 cup of the pasta cooking water).

In a large sauté pan, warm the bean sauce, add the pasta and beans and toss gently, adding pasta water to moisten, if needed. Sprinkle with grated Pecorino Romano cheese and freshly ground black pepper, to taste.

Linguine al pesto

Serves 4

2 cloves garlic
2 cups fresh basil, cleaned and stems removed
3 tbs pine nuts
1/2 teaspoon salt
1/2 cup olive oil
1 tbs chopped Italian parsley
1 lbs thin linguine pasta
4 tbs grated Pecorino Romano

Combine the first 6 ingredients in a food processor at medium speed for 3 to 4 minutes. Set aside.
In a large saucepan or stock pot, bring 4 quarts of water to a boil. Cook the linguine in the boiling water for 4 or 5 minutes or until pasta is just done. (Reserve a little of boiling water and set aside). Drain the pasta and return it to the pot. Add the sauce to the pasta and combine.

If the pasta is a bit dry, add a little of the reserved water.
Add the Pecorino Romano cheese, combine and serve.

Roman-style tripe

Serves 4

2 lbs pre-cooked tripe
2 onions
2 carrots
1 stick celery
2 cloves

2 16 oz. cans tomato purée
1-1/2 oz. pork fat or dripping
3 tbs extra virgin olive oil
1 tbs mint leaves
1 lb grated Pecorino Romano
Salt

To prepare the sauce, gently sauté in olive oil one finely sliced onion, one diced carrot and half the stick of celery. Add the fat, and after a minute or two, the tomato purée, salt to taste and cook over a moderate heat for 30 minutes.

In a large pan of water, place the remaining carrot, celery and the onion spiked with the cloves. Season with salt and when the water boils add the washed tripe that has been chopped into squares. After five minutes, drain tripe, cut into narrow strips and cook in the sauce for 30 minutes.
Remove the pan from the heat, add the mint and mix well. Serve the tripe in a heated dish drizzled with the grated Pecorino Romano cheese.

Maccarrones de busa

(Sardinian oven-baked bucatini pasta)

Serves 4

1 lb bucatini pasta
16 oz. can tomato purée
2 tbs grated Pecorino Romano
2 tbs fresh Pecorino Romano, diced
1 lb fresh Pecorino Romano, flaked
1 clove garlic
1 tbs chopped parsley
1 carrot
1 stick celery
3 tbs extra virgin olive oil
Salt

Place the olive oil, garlic, celery, carrot, parsley and tomato purée in a large shallow pan, season with salt and cook for 30 minutes in order to obtain a thin sauce. Cook the bucatini in a large pan of salted boiling water. Drain when just tender and put in the pan with the tomato sauce from which garlic, celery and carrot have been removed. Add the grated and diced Pecorino Romano cheese and mix well. Put the mixture in an oven-proof dish, drizzle on top the flakes of Pecorino Romano cheese and place in a moderate oven (350° F.) for 3/4 minutes and serve immediately.

Bombas e casu

(meatballs with Pecorino Romano cheese)

Serves 4

1 lb mixed minced meat (beef, veal, pork)
2 tbs grated Pecorino Romano
2 thin slices fresh Pecorino Romano
1 clove chopped garlic
1/2 onion, thinly sliced
1 tbs chopped parsley
A little flour
4 tbs extra virgin olive oil
1/2 glass white wine

Mix the minced meat together with the grated cheese, garlic, onion, parsley and a pinch of salt. Form into small meat balls no bigger than a walnut, roll them in flour and sauté in olive oil. Add the wine and continue cooking over a low heat until sauce is reduced.

Place the slices of fresh cheese in an oven-proof dish, add the cooked meatballs and the rest of the sauce. Place in a moderately heated oven for a few minutes until the Pecorino Romano cheese starts to melt. Serve immediately.

Cacio e pepe
(pasta with Pecorino Romano and pepper)

Serves 4

1 cup Pecorino Romano
4 level teaspoons freshly ground black pepper
1 lb fusilli pasta
2 tablespoons extra virgin olive oil

Use it in mouth-watering dishes that are easy to prepare and good to look at, just like the one pictured below. Put the Pecorino Romano cheese in a large bowl and toss with the pepper (there should be enough pepper flecks to speckle the cheese). In a large pan, bring to the boil 5 quarts of salted water, add the fusilli and cook until just done. Drain the fusilli, keep aside 3/4 cup of the boiling water.

Add the fusilli to the bowl of cheese and toss, adding a little of the water if needed to keep the fusilli moist. Drizzle with olive oil and serve.

Pizza with Pecorino Romano cheese and onions

Serves 4

Pizza dough

1 lb flour
1 oz. yeast
2 tbs extra virgin olive oil

Topping

2 lbs white onions
8 tbs grated Pecorino Romano
3 tbs chopped parsley
1 tbs marjoram and thyme leaves
4 tbs extra virgin olive oil

Mix the flour with a pinch of salt, a little of the olive oil, and the yeast dissolved in a glass of tepid water. Knead into a smooth dough and roll into a ball. Place the dough in a bowl and cover with a cloth and leave to rise for about 2 hours. Peel and lightly boil the onions, drain them well, slice thinly and set aside. Knead the dough again, roll out and place on a greased baking tray and leave to rise again. Spread the olive oil, grated cheese, onions, marjoram and thyme on the pasta dough and season with salt. Bake in a moderately hot (200° F.) oven for about 30 minutes. Drizzle with parsley and serve.

The sweets

Pecorino Romano cream

Grate a cup of grated Pecorino Romano cheese and blend with whipped cream. Place in an ovenproof dish and cook in a double boiler in the oven until the cream thickens. Cool and serve with chilled white wine.

Ravioli with Pecorino Romano cheese

Make a dough using white flour, shortening, sugar, egg yolk, brandy, white wine and salt. Knead and roll out to the thickness of a coin. Using a tumbler, cut into disks and on each one place a spoonful of a mixture composed of grated Pecorino Romano cheese, egg-white, brandy, orange essence and, if desired, grated nutmeg. Dampen the outer edges of the ravioli disks and fold over in a half-moon shape and bake for a few minutes on a floured baking tray. When just beginning to take on a pale-blond color, remove from heat and leave to cool. Serve with a glass of chilled dry white wine.

Pecorino Romano cheese crepes

Make the crepes by mixing into a dough white flour, sugar, water, white wine and a pinch of salt. Roll out thinly. Fry the crepes in vegetable oil using a Blinis pan. Turn over and sprinkle with grated Pecorino Romano cheese, continuing cooking until cheese melts. Fold in four and serve hot.

Pecorino Romano cheese crepes with aromatic syrup

Make the crepes as above except that the grated Pecorino Romano cheese is added at the start in the dough mixture. Once the crepes are fried, spread them with a syrup made from brown sugar, dry white wine and powdered ginger.

continued from page 40

hand by craftsmen known by special names that denote their role. These expert workers are as eagerly sought after as were the great master craftsmen who made furniture and musical instruments in the 17th century.

The results of their endeavors are shown in the following table of the composition for 100 grams (3.5 ounces) of Pecorino Romano cheese as sold in grocery stores and supermarkets:

Humidity 32%

Fats 31-32%

Protein 25%

Minerals (phosphorous, calcium, potassium, magnesium) 4%

Vitamins A-B-C-D-E

the Roman poet Virgil referred to the soldiers partaking of an "uncia" of Pecorino a day to sustain them in their conquests for the Roman Empire

Vitamins A-D are particularly important for the formation and growth of bone and this explains why Pecorino Romano is recommended for nursing mothers and, through them, for newborn babies.

But Pecorino Romano is not only considered advisable for growing youngsters. Back in ancient times it formed an important part of the daily rations of the Roman legions and the Roman poet Virgil referred to the soldiers partaking of an "uncia", or ounce, of Pecorino a day which they added to a mush of wheat grains to sustain them in their conquests for the Roman Empire.

A nutritional table prepared recently by international experts and accepted by the

Italian Nutrition Institute recommends the following daily intake:

Protein	60 grams
Fats	72 grams
Carbohydrates	380 grams

Comparing the table with the rations drawn up by the unknown Roman nutritionist of 2,000 years ago, we see that he came surprisingly close to the dietary dictates of today indicating that Pecorino Romano is of great value as part of regular meals in a healthily-balanced Mediterranean diet. Of course the Roman soldiers knew nothing about balanced diets or nutrition, they were simply grateful for the morsel of cheese that lent flavor to their unpalatable mush of boiled grains. And how many weight watchers in modern times have discovered that Pecorino Romano grated onto a salad makes it more appetising without upsetting their diet? According to the teaching of a renowned Salerno medical school in the Middle

" Pecorino Romano is of great value as part of regular meals in a healthily-balanced Mediterranean diet. "

Ages:
"Bread and cheese are good foods for healthy mankind ... ignorant physicians put cheese among those things bad

for us. But they do not know in what way cheese is bad for us; cheese stimulates an exhausted stomach into action if consumed after a meal by helping to digest the other foods that have been eaten. This can be verified by anybody who knows physics."

Pecorino Romano cheese owes much of its presence on the North American market to the inhabitants of Little Italy in New York. Once these newcomers originating from central and southern Italy settled in and prospered, they began to introduce elements of their own culture through the arts, religion and, naturally, through food and flavors. So it was that on saint days and national holidays, Pecorino Romano was part of the festive spread along with pure olive oil, plum tomatoes and the typical honey- and ricotta-filled confectionery of southern Italy. Importation of Pecorino Romano to the U.S. was only sporadic until the end of the 19th century and was a casual transaction oper- ated by the grocers of Little Italy using family and friendship links, but without any official guarantee of size, shape or, above all, quality.

But business boomed as the life style of the Italo-American community improved and by the turn of the century the commerce of

Pecorino Romano owes much of its presence on the North American market to the inhabitants of Little Italy in New York

Pecorino Romano was modernized, quality had become constant and the quantity imported was on an industrial scale. In 1910, no less than 16.5 million pounds were imported into the U.S. But to satisfy this demand, the dairy farms round Rome found they were short of sheep, grazing lands and operatives. Looking round for a new zone in which to expand production, the island of Sardinia, with its traditional sheep-rearing tradition, was an almost natural choice. Grazing lands were plentiful and well-provided with sweet-smelling aromatic grass. The quality of the sheep's milk obtained from Sardinian sheep was not dissimular to that of the breed in Lazio. At this point, the Societa' Casearia Romana, headquarters of Pecorino Romano production,

" Looking round for a new zone in which to expand production, the island of Sardinia was an almost natural choice "

Tourists visiting Italy also helped to spread the word and increase the popularity of the cheese

was transferred to Sardinia along with the skilled cheese makers and the modern machinery used in the conversion of sheep's milk. Other dairy farmers followed, Sardinian entrepreneurs joined in and by 1955, when the law prescribing production methods was passed, it was decided to retain the traditional Roman name due to its historical importance and the technology involved even though production by that time was 80% Sardinian.

The success story of Pecorino Romano as an export for the American market has had its fluctuations, particularly during the First and Second World Wars, but continued to expand when the Italo-American community began to spread throughout America taking with them their preference for the Pecorino Romano cheese of their origins thanks to its remarkable quality consistency. Imitations, which still exist, could not stand up to the unfailingly high standard of the original cheese and so only managed to corner the lower end of the market without giving any trouble to genuine Pecorino Romano.

Tourists visiting Italy also helped to spread the word and increase the popularity of the

cheese as did the many articles in the foreign press singing the praises of Italian cooking. Today Pecorino Romano is exported in consistent quantities to Germany, Holland, Switzerland and France even though these do not match up to the spectacular sales to the New World.

Pecorino Romano is a cheese that has stood the test of time over thousands of years. Its characteristics have been fine-tuned even though it is still produced using centuries-old techniques, while abiding strictly by internationally-required hygiene standards and the use of modern industrial equipment. Based on sheep's milk, a raw material that is close to nature, modern from the nutritional point of view with unmistakable characteristics of firm consistency, taste and aroma, Pecorino Romano is guaranteed by

" Pecorino Romano is a cheese that has stood the test of time over thousands of years "

the authenticity stamp of a Consortium that grants it only to products that match up to extremely high standards.

What can we do with a raw material of this type? This is not the silly question that it seems to be. Certainly we eat Pecorino Romano in the springtime with raw fava beans, also it teams well sprinkled on the classical pasta dishes of Rome and its surroundings and of southern Italy (such as all'amatriciana, alla carbonara, alla Gricia, or cheese and pepper); it is delicious too as an accompaniment to typical Sardinian dishes (pane fratau, maccarrones de busa, bombas); it can be grated on cooked tripe dishes and it is good too used in Genoese pesto sauce. It can be served in chunks at table and it is the basic element in one of the oldest forms of Neapolitan pizza. These are all exceptionally tasty recipes and many will be mentioned in this book. But does pecorino have a place in the evolution of modern cookery? Is this a creative moment which today, more than ever, in Italy and elsewhere, characterizes gastronomy?

Only great cheeses can be successfully included in cooking

To find an answer, it is necessary to clarify

a concept, which entails eliminating certain prejudices radicated in the culinary mentality, both professional and non-professional. When a cheese used in cooking is part of the elaboration and cooking of a complex dish, subconsciously it is considered as a simple ingredient to be grated. But it should be emphasized that only great cheeses can be included in cooking and very few cheeses are so wonderful as to be equally good in both a casserole and also served uncooked during the same meal. It is only those few cheeses that reach these heights that can be described as "gastronomic" and Pecorino Romano enters into this category. It has the virtue of not becoming stringy when cooked, a quality greatly appreciated by chefs, in order not to alter the consistency of the dish.

"But obviously the most important quality Pecorino Romano has to possess is its flavor"

But obviously the most important quality pecorino has to possess is flavor which, as we have already mentioned, is unaltered by cooking. This makes it possible to team it, even daringly, with other ingredients.

Pecorino Romano does not become stringy when cooked and so does not alter the consistency of the dish

According to cooking theories, you can team a flavor provided it is distinct, either to a like or a contrasting flavor. So let's take a look at which might be the ideal companions for Pecorino Romano, both in one sense and the other.

The contrast is the easiest to achieve. It might be the teaming of a nugget of pecorino to nibble with a fresh ripe pear or perhaps pecorino with honey (an exquisite dessert that is gaining in popularity consists of a slice of Pecorino Romano with bitter corbezzolo honey washed down with a good Marsala wine, an aged Samperi or even a good Tawny port.) Still on the subject of contrasts, I am a firm believer in a gratin of sweet-tasting greens (such as fennel, leeks, or potatoes with Tropea onions) in which Pecorino Romano holds the gratin together. I find interesting the typically Apulian combination of a tasty fish like pagello sprinkled with a veil of the cheese that forms a crusty surface when baked in the oven. And the union of a delicately flavored dairy product like ricotta with a hint of Pecorino Romano in some dishes is worthy of consideration.

Linking Pecorino Romano to a similar flavor works best when using small quantities of the cheese alongside other mild flavors so that they exalt each other. In this sense there are many traditional pasta recipes, such as cheese and pepper and all'amatriciana, or the cheese combined with various sauces based on minced beef or lamb, or used on white pizza with onions. Or there are the many interesting regional dishes like the Apulian open tart with sardines or anchovies seasoned with herbs with which Pecorino Romano forms a fascinating symbiosis. And I am also convinced that some of the traditional Sardinian dishes like "Suppa Quatta" or "alla Gallurese" consisting of layers of fresh sheep's milk cheese and bread in meat broth, would be improved by the addition of a few flakes of Pecorino Romano.

The recipes are intended as an invitation to both professional and amateur cooks to think with the flavor of Pecorino Romano

Piazza Navona

CONSORZIO PER LA TUTELA
DEL FORMAGGIO PECORINO ROMANO

C.so Umberto I, 226 - 08015 MACOMER (NU) - ITALY

Produced by:
Grapho
Marketing & Communication

Cover photo: "Sheep on Via Appia", Alinari Archive
Illustrations: Alessio Coppola
Food photos: Armando Zuppa
Photos of Pecorino Romano production: Enrico Blasi
Edited by Diadelos - Printed in Italy
© 1994 - Italian Consortium for Pecorino Romano cheese

This book is a complimentary copy by courtesy of
the Italian Consortium for Pecorino Romano cheese
and the Italian Ministry of Agriculture, Food and Forest Resources